ISLAND OF PALMAS CASE: THE UNITED STATES OF AMERICA VS THE NETHERLANDS

VOLUME 2, ISSUE 4 OF BRILLOPEDIA

HARPREET SINGH MALHOTRA

Made with ❤ on the Notion Press Platform
www.notionpress.com

Contents

Preface

"Start writing, no matter what. The water does not flow until the faucet is turned on".

- Louis L'Amour

Hundreds of students and professors are contributing their work to Brillopedia, we are here to provide ample information about Law and Contemporary issues. Our aim is to provide a platform for today's generation to express their views and ideas on law and contemporary law.

Author

Harpreet Singh Malhotra

CHAPTER ONE

ABSTRACT

The Island of Palmas case stands as a landmark case of International law dealing with territorial dispute between two subjects of International law. Under this case, the dispute was resolved by the way of Arbitration between the parties that is The United States of America as 'The Claimant' and The Netherlands as 'The Respondent'. The dispute was instituted in "Permanent Court of Arbitration". The citation of the case is Perm. Ct. Arb. 1928. The Arbitrator involved in this case was "Mr. Max Huber". The arbitration award was announced on 04th April 1928.

"Palmas is an island of little economic value or strategic location which is located is 2.6 km in north–south length and 1.0 km in east–west width. In the year 1932 the island of Palmas had a population of about 750. The Island of Palmas is located in the southernmost part of the Philippines and the north most part of Indonesia.

FACTS

In January 1925 the United States of America filed a land dispute on the sovereignty of Island of Palmas against the Netherlands in the Permanent court of Arbitration.

• Both The United States of America and the Netherlands claimed that the sovereignty over the Island of Palmas.

• The claim of the United States to sovereignty over the Island of Palmas is derived from the "Rights by Discovery" as the Spanish explorers had discovered the Island of Palmas first.

• In 1898, the war between Spain and United States of America came to an end and it resulted in the signing of "The Treaty of Paris, 1898".

• The Treaty of Paris 1898 provided that the Spanish territories ceded to the United States of America. Moreover, the United States of America contended that Spanish ceded its territory of Philippines which included the Island of Palmas.

• The Netherlands also claimed sovereignty of the Island of Palmas on the basic of series of contracts signed by the Netherlands and The East India Company between 1677 and 1899.

• According to the Respondent, the Netherlands, the Island of Palmas was considered as a part of East Indian dominion which is under the Dutch sovereignty.

• The Netherlands based their arguments on the basis of "Rights of continuous and peaceful displays of sovereignty" in which they contended that East Indian Company specifically listed the Island of Palmas as a part of the Dutch Frontiers. Moreover, the contract of East India Company outlined the provisions for working and regulating of the Island of Palmas's economy.

CHAPTER THREE

ISSUSE

This case involves couple of issues which relates to possession over a territory and applicability of doctrine of continuous and peaceful display of sovereignty over a territory. The issues are specifically stated here asunder —

1. The prime issue involved in this case is that who is the rightful owner of the territory of Island of Palma?

2. The other issue involved in this case is that can a claim which is in Choate prevail over a definite claim found upon the continuous and peaceful display of sovereignty?

CHAPTER FOUR

LAW APPLIED

1. Convention for the Pacific Settlement of International Disputes 1907: The Convention provided frameworks for resolving international disputes by the following means –

• By establishing a conciliation commission under Articles 1 to 16;

• By establishing an arbitration tribunal under Articles 21 to 28;

• By deferring the failed disputes to the Permanent Court of International Justice under Article 17 to 20;

"Thus, by combining all three different 'model convention' proposals from the League's Commission of Arbitration and Security - set up by the League's Preparation Commission in 1927 - into one unified act."

2. Treaty of Paris, 1898: The Treaty of Paris was signed in the year 1898 on 10th of December for the purpose of making a peace agreement between two international subject namely as Spain and the United States for ending the Spanish-American War. The treaty of Paris 1898 was a significant importance as Cuba gained independence from Spain. Moreover the United States of America gained possession over the territory of the Philippines, Puerto Rico, and Guam. The Treaty successfully ended Spanish imperialism and establish the United States of America as a world power in terms of position.

3. East India Company contracts (1677 - 1899): There were an existence list of binding contracts between East India Company and the Netherlands which aimed at providing the provisions for regulating the economic activities of Palmas Island.

4. Doctrine of Continuous and peaceful display of sovereignty: Doctrine of continuous and peaceful display of sovereignty talks about that the territorial sovereignty of State can be established or identified on the basis of continuing and peacefully functioning of sovereign activities in the territory. The principle that there exists a continuous and peaceful

exhibition of the functioning of international Subject / State within a given province is a constituent element of territorial sovereignty. Further territorial sovereignty of a State is not based solely on the condition that it is formed as an independent State and their boundaries but also on the conditions of international jurisprudence and doctrine widely accepted across the global.

CHAPTER FIVE

DECISION

The Permanent Court of Arbitration in this case awarded that he sovereignty of Island of Palmas in the favour of the Netherlands. The Permanent Court of Arbitration ruled that the American claim to rule by discovery failed to prove due to lack of evidence that Spanish administration or possession over Islands of Palmas. The Permanent Court of Arbitration ruled that the Netherlands had successfully established the Islands as part of the Sangihe Islands displaying continuous and peace display of sovereignty and confirming the legality over the title.

The Arbitrator stated the following –

"The arbitrator concluded that even if it had been possible for Spain to have ceded to the United States of America its inchoate title derived from discovery or contiguity the inchoate title of the Netherlands could not have been modified by a treaty concluded by third Powers; and such a treaty could not have impressed the character of illegality on any act undertaken by the Netherlands with a view to completing their inchoate title... at least as long as no dispute on the matter had arisen. By the time a dispute had arisen, in 1906, the arbitrator found that the establishment of Dutch authority had already reached such a degree of development, that the importance of maintaining this state of things ought to be considered as prevailing over a claim, possibly based either on discovery in very distant times and unsupported by occupation or mere geographical position. For these reasons, the arbitrator held that the Island of Palmas (or Miangas) formed in its entirety a part of Netherlands territory."

CHAPTER SIX

ANALYSIS

This international case is surely a landmark case as it set outs two precedents which are highlighted below

1. Titles founded upon right by discovery are deemed inchoate.

2. When another sovereign begins to exercise continuous and actual sovereignty and the discoverer of such territory does not contest the claim then the claim by the sovereign that exercises authority is greater than sovereignty which is based on discovery.

CHAPTER SEVEN

CONCLUSION

The case is one of the most influential precedents dealing with island territorial conflicts. The essential point is therefore to make up your mind whether Spain had sovereignty over island of Palmas at the time of the approaching into force of the Treaty of Paris. The United States base their claim on the titles of discovery, of recognition by treaty and of contiguity, i.e. titles referring to acts or circumstances leading to the acquisition of sovereignty; they need to however not able to established the fact that sovereignty so acquired was effectively displayed at any time. The Netherlands based their arguments on the basis of "Rights of continuous and peaceful displays of sovereignty" in which they contended that East Indian Company specifically listed the Island of Palmas as a part of the Dutch Frontiers. Moreover, the contract of East India Company outlined the provisions for working and regulating of the island of Palmas's economy. This resulted within the display of undisturbed sovereignty by the Dutch.